HERE COMES THE BRIDE
- WORSHIP UNFOLDED

Here Comes the Bride - Worship Unfolded

Apostles Lamont & Tiffany Bigham

ETERNALink
~ PUBLISHING ~

Scripture quotations are taken from the following translations:
English Standard Version (ESV) – Scripture quotations are from *The Holy Bible, English Standard Version®, ESV®*, copyright © 2001 by Crossway, a publishing ministry of Good News Publishers. Used by permission. All rights reserved.
God's Word Translation (GW) – Scripture taken from *God's Word®*, copyright © 1995 by God's Word to the Nations. Used by permission. All rights reserved.
Amplified Bible (AMP) – Scripture quotations taken from the *Amplified® Bible*, copyright © 2015 by The Lockman Foundation. Used by permission. All rights reserved. www.lockman.org
New International Version (NIV) – Scripture taken from the *Holy Bible, New International Version®, NIV®*, copyright © 1973, 1978, 1984, 2011 by Biblica, Inc.® Used by permission. All rights reserved worldwide.
King James Version (KJV) – Scripture quotations from the *King James Version (KJV)* are in the public domain.

Eternalink Publishing, 2025

Contents

DEDICATION

To our loving parents—thank you for being the first examples of strength, faith, and unconditional love. Your legacy continues to shape our journey.

To our incredible children—your lives are a daily reminder of God's promises and our greatest assignment. May you always walk in truth and worship boldly.

To our family & friends —your support, encouragement, and prayers have been a sustaining force in our lives and ministry. We are better because of you.

And to every Kingdom co-laborer we've had the privilege to serve with, and to those who have ever deposited into, mentored, or invested in our lives—this is also your fruit. Thank you for seeing us, believing in us, and helping shape our "yes." May this book reflect the impact of every seed you've sown.

1

Introduction

Here Comes the Bride - Worship Unfolded
By: Apostles Lamont & Tiffany Bigham

In the heart of every Christian, there exists a sacred longing—a profound desire to stand in the presence of the Divine, to offer adoration and gratitude, and to partake in a celestial union. This longing transcends the boundaries of time and place, weaving a tapestry of worship that spans generations and cultures. It is a timeless love story, the spiritual romance of humanity and its Creator, where the bride—His beloved people—prepares to meet the Groom. This book, "Here Comes the Bride," is an invitation to step into this sacred journey, a journey that unfolds in the hallowed corridors of Christian worship.

As the pages of this book turn, we will venture deep into the heart of this sacred love story, exploring the facets of worship that reveal the profound connection between the Creator and His creation. Christian worship, in its essence, is not a mere routine or tradition; it is the sacred dialogue between heaven and earth, a dance of the heart and soul, where the worshiper becomes the bride, and God the Bridegroom.

Through the ages, Christians have gathered in diverse settings, from magnificent cathedrals adorned with stained-glass to simple, humble chapels, from ornate sanctuaries to open fields, and even within the quiet corners of their own homes. It's in these sacred spaces and moments that the bride, the Church, readies herself to meet the Groom. This book delves into the elements that form the very fabric of this spiritual courtship, offering insights, revelations, and inspiration to enrich the worshiper's encounter with the Divine.

"Here Comes the Bride" celebrates the rich tapestry of Christian worship. It shines a light on the significance of tradition and innovation, the beauty of liturgy and spontaneity, the power of community and solitude—all woven together in a harmonious symphony that resonates with the heavens.

As we journey through these pages, we will discover the intricate details of worship's grand design—the rich symbolism, the biblical foundations, and the profound spiritual truths that are etched into its very core. Together, we will explore the fragrance of incense, the power of the Word, the grace of the sacraments, and the transformative potential of true worship.

Join us on this journey as we unveil the beauty of Christian worship—the timeless narrative of the Bride drawing near to her Bridegroom. It is a story that transcends time, culture, and circumstance, offering solace and inspiration to the believer and seeker alike. "Here Comes the Bride" is not just a book; it is an invitation to participate in this sacred love story, to draw closer to the One who is both the source and the destination of our deepest longings.

2

Dominion

Dominion defined in Dictionary.com is the power or right of governing and controlling: sovereign authority. The God – given ability to rule over, to have supremacy in, to be in charge of, to command and direct that what God has given us.

Let's look at this from the very beginning of the beginning of time in the Book of Genesis in the history of creation when God created a being called mankind, in Genesis chapter 2 verse 7. But, starting in verses 15 – 25 in chapter 2, man was given authority and legal right by God to name, tend to, dwell in (live), pasture, and to be with God because of his heart, the intentions to be with man and His creation, the purpose and goal of God was to create something for Himself. Man and God were inseparable and connected in such a way that the supernatural did take place when God made Adam and when He put Adam asleep, to make woman. They were to rule and cover the territory, the space, the dwelling place together in the presence of an Almighty God. They could just worship and be with Him. You see, God always had His intentions for making, creating, and designing us, we are for Him, made for Him to enjoy.

Two scriptures come to mind as we write this revelation of God's intent. The first scripture is in Revelation 4:11 GW: "Our Lord and God, you deserve to receive glory, honor, and power because you created everything. Everything came into existence and was created because of your will." God wanted us in His presence, in His glory abiding with Him. The next scripture is in Psalm 147:11 GW: It says, "The Lord is pleased with those who fear him, with those who wait with hope for his mercy." God Himself delights in what He has made, we can praise Him, so He is happy about that. We can worship like the original thought that the Divine Council had in the very idea that was drawn up from heaven to earth, genuinely and wholeheartedly glorifying Him.

This chapter is an exploration of what it means to be a worshiper who embraces the concept of dominion, not as an assertion of power or control, but as a sacred responsibility and privilege.

DOMINION OVER CREATION

From the dawn of creation, humanity was given dominion over the earth. In the book of Genesis, we read, "Then God said, 'Let us make man in our image, after our likeness. And let them have dominion over the fish of the sea and over the birds of the heavens and over the livestock and over all the earth and over every creeping thing that creeps on the earth.'" (Genesis 1:26, ESV). This dominion was not a mandate for exploitation but a call to stewardship, a sacred trust to care for the earth and its creatures.

As worshipers, we recognize that dominion over creation is intertwined with our devotion to God. The very act of worship is an acknowledgment of God's sovereignty as the Creator, and our role as stewards of His creation. This dominion extends beyond physical landscapes to encompass the spiritual realm, where we are called to exercise authority over the forces of darkness through prayer, intercession, and the power of God's Word

DOMINION OVER SELF

Another aspect of Christian dominion involves mastery over one's own self. The Apostle Paul wrote, "But I discipline my body and keep it under control, lest after preaching to others I myself should be disqualified." (1 Corinthians 9:27, ESV). This dominion is the spiritual discipline of self-control, where we yield to the Holy Spirit, allowing God to rule over our desires, thoughts, and actions.

As worshipers, we recognize that surrender is the path to dominion over self. In worship, we offer ourselves as living sacrifices, allowing God's transformative power to renew our minds and sanctify our hearts. Dominion over self is not about tyranny, but about submitting to the gentle rule of a loving and wise God, who shapes us into vessels of His grace.

DOMINION IN THE WORLD

As worshipers, we are not called to retreat from the world, but to engage with it. Jesus spoke of a different kind of dominion when He said, "Go therefore and make disciples of all nations..." (Matthew 28:19, ESV). This dominion is the Great Commission—the call to be ambassadors of God's love, grace, and reconciliation.

Our dominion in the world is an expression of worship. It is through acts of kindness, justice, and compassion that we demonstrate the love of God. We carry the message of salvation, offering others the opportunity to become worshipers themselves. Dominion in the world is not about imposing our will, but about extending God's kingdom through humility, love, and servanthood.

DOMINION AS WORSHIP

In the grand narrative of Christian worship, dominion is not an exercise of human strength or authority; it is a posture of reverence and obedience to the One we worship. As worshipers, we understand that dominion is not an end in itself, but a means to fulfill God's redemptive plan for creation.

In dominion, we embody the values of God's kingdom, reflecting His character and extending His love. Our dominion is an offering of worship—a recognition that all authority, power, and glory ultimately belong to God. It is a declaration that His dominion is our delight, and in embracing our role as stewards, disciples, and ambassadors, we find our true purpose and fulfillment as worshipers. Dominion, when grounded in humility and reverence, becomes a powerful act of worship, a harmonious symphony in the grand chorus of Christian devotion.

3

The Dwelling Place

As we stand on the threshold of Christian worship, a question emerges—a question that has echoed through the corridors of faith for millennia: Where does God dwell? Is there a specific place, a sacred space, where the Divine presence is most profoundly felt? The answer, it seems, is woven into the very fabric of worship itself, for the idea of a "dwelling place" holds a special significance in the Christian journey.

THE GARDEN

Heaven and earth collided at this moment, and it all just wrapped in one, it became synchronized and compatible for the glory of the Father. The image and what was spoken between Divine Council in heaven came into pure existence. God needed a place, a space, a sanctuary to meet with man and commune with Him whenever and wherever in the Garden. God would literally come down and inhabit this place in His fullness and power, and rest in such a place of natural beauty and paradise. This place was holy, which really now made Adam and Eve types of priests before a holy God, exercising dominion over all that God gave them. They cultivated and kept this place holy for God at this time. We are all priests for God, created to worship before Him, a kingdom of priest (Exodus 19:6). We are defined and described as royal and a holy people according to 1 Peter 2:5, 9. Authentic worship was erected and established from the beginning of time. This existence of mankind still being in a place, in a position as such has been restored unto us again. The fall was done, but Jesus Christ made it a FINISHED WORK!! We are heirs of Christ, we are His inheritance and heritage, and He wants us just like we should want Him.

THE TENT MEETING

In the ancient wilderness, when the Israelites embarked on their Exodus from Egypt, they were led by a pillar of cloud by day and fire by night. The guiding presence of God led them to a place where they would construct the Tent of Meeting, also known as the Tabernacle. This portable sanctuary was a dwelling place for God among His people. It was a place of worship, sacrifice, and divine encounter, a precursor to the grand temples of Jerusalem.

The significance of the Tabernacle was not just in its architectural details but in what it represented—a place where the Divine met mankind, where heaven and earth converged. It was a space designed for relationship, for communion, for worship.

THE CONSTRUCTION OF THE TEMPLE

According to Exodus Chapters 31-39, God gives plans to Moses for the design and also certain people that he wanted to use as instruments to build the house of worship, but HIS way and NOT man's way. God wanted a place to dwell, a place for himself to be worshiped. The first person God mentioned was someone named Bezalel. Bezalel name means "in the shadow (protection) of God." He was responsible for the holy oils, incense and holy garments. The next person was Oholiab. Oholiab name means "father's tent"

He was master of carpentry and temple furniture. He worked under Bezalel. Chapter 31 specifically explains the duties and operations for all involved in the construction. Bezalel was a foreman, a builder, a craftsman builder of the Tabernacle, appointed by God to build and was known to have the legacy of a godly family. He belonged to the tribe of Judah. Bezalel was filled in {EX. 31} with the spirit of God to build / construct, and he crafted God's house the way he wanted it! Wow! They made the Tabernacle "for God" "For him" to dwell. The same Holy Spirit that "inspired" the writings of the Holy word, filled Bezalel to create / build the temple. He was inspired by the Holy Spirit to do an assignment led by Him! The Holy Spirit can come upon you to get wisdom, knowledge, and understanding fulfilling an assignment just like Bezalel. Bezalel made furniture for God! Each piece!

- The throne that "God" will sit upon! Wow! He makes the seat.
- Creating a place for God, the Triune to sit, a place for him to sit. What was Bezalel thinking? I wonder?
- Bezalel making the incense altar that goes to God straight to him from us.
- Intimate worship tools created by Bezalel - in the shadow of God. Psalm 91:1 says, "Whoever lives under the shelter of the Most High will remain in the shadow of the Almighty."

THE TEMPLE IN JERUSALEM

In time, the Tabernacle gave way to the grand Temple in Jerusalem, a place of unparalleled beauty and majesty. The Temple was constructed with meticulous care, adorned with precious metals, stones, and intricate carvings. It was where the Ark of the Covenant resided, and it became the heart of worship. But beyond its grandeur, it served as a symbol of God's dwelling among His people.

The Temple was a place where God's presence was believed to dwell in a special way. It was the center of worship, a home, a sacrifice, and solemn gathering. It was within its sacred walls that devout men and women encountered the Divine, found forgiveness, and experienced His grace.

THE NEW COVENANT DWELLING

In God's Kingdom, the idea of a dwelling place takes on a new and profound meaning. With the life, death, and resurrection of Jesus Christ, the dwelling place of God is no longer confined to a physical structure but expands to encompass the hearts of believers. In the New Covenant, the Apostle Paul tells us, "Do you not know that your bodies are temples of the Holy Spirit?" (1 Corinthians 6:19).

This truth transforms the way we perceive worship. The dwelling place of God is no longer a fixed location but a dwelling within the human heart. When believers gather in the name of Christ, they become the living stones of a spiritual temple, offering their worship as living sacrifices (Romans 12:1). It is here, in the hearts and lives of believers, that God's presence is most profoundly felt, and worship becomes an intimate encounter with the Divine.

Our desire and passion to create and cultivate such a place is NOW!! We must create and establish "GLORY" all over thus world. Freely carrying the glory of God inside of us to bear heaven on earth, like in the Garden of Eden. For Jesus said in Luke 9:58,

Jesus told him, "Foxes have holes, and birds have nests, but the Son of Man has nowhere to sleep." Can we make a place as David did to lay his head? To make a home, a sanctuary, a habitation for Him to dwell, to live. You know, the scripture in Luke 9, Jesus gave this statement to make a point about when you truly surrender to the Lord and say yes to Him that it's a lifestyle of abandon and selflessness for the cause of the kingdom. Times in worship at our varies places of worship or churches or ministries, we don't plan to really spend time with the Lord in His presence in a space, sanctuary, or a place for Him to come and just dwell. We make it a place just to come and enjoy, but then He, the Spirit, is grieved by our intent. He still wants to dwell and build a HABITATION and not just what so many of us are used to, just a VISITATION.

THE DWELLING PLACE TODAY

In today's world, Christian worship can be expressed in grand cathedrals, humble chapels, contemporary church buildings, and even in homes. It can be marked by traditional liturgy, charismatic expressions, or a blend of both. But the essence of the dwelling place remains the same—it is where God's people gather in His name, and His presence dwells among them.

The Tent of Meeting, the Temple in Jerusalem, and the temple of believers are all interconnected in the story of Christian worship. They represent a trajectory of God's desire to dwell among His people, from the physical to the spiritual, from the ancient to the modern.

In this chapter, we have explored the concept of the dwelling place in Christian worship, tracing its origins, transformations, and significance. The dwelling place of God is a reminder that we are never alone in our worship. Whether in the quiet moments of personal devotion or the exuberant gatherings of the faithful, God is present, dwelling among us. The true Temple is not built with stones but with hearts aflame with love and devotion, for in our worship, we become the dwelling place of the Divine.

4

Sounds of God's Heart

In the grand symphony of Christian worship, there is a melody that resounds above all others—the sound of God's heart. This chapter is an exploration of the profound notion that worship is not only about what we offer to God but also about what we receive from Him—the sounds of His heart.

Do we really listen and hear the Father's heart? The rhythm and beats that take us straight to Him. Setting a prophetic and apostolic stage for Him to come. Times of releasing certain sounds, beats, prophetic acts and rhythms from an anointed minstrel, or even vocal sounds will provoke the presence of God to come and dwell with us, His people!!

We believe one of the best examples in the bible of someone provoking the presence of God for the supernatural; was David. One of David's skillful and cunning dimensions was he knew how to get God's attention by playing certain chords and notes. The striking from his hands to the instrument would allow the supernatural to take place wherever and for whoever needed to receive it. The best example was David's playing for Saul. In 1 Samuel

16:22-23 GW, it says "Saul sent this message to Jesse, "Please let David stay with me because I have grown fond of him. Whenever God's spirit came to Saul, David took the lyre and strummed a tune. Saul got relief from his terror and felt better, and the evil spirit left him." David had the calling, anointing and dominion to play certain notes that would provoke the supernatural move of atmosphere, realms, and even spirits from Saul. David provokes to change what even God was allowing; an evil spirit to be moved to a place of life. Why would God allow a mere man to have this type of favor and dominion? When God calls and anoints, he freely gives that person the ability to move in their gifting, authority and dominion for the supernatural. This is a perfect example of the Dominion of Worship for the Supernatural.

What we have learned and experienced through our anointing to move in worship has been beyond unbelievable. We have seen people free from demons, healed and cured supernaturally from just elevating our worship to God beyond our natural understanding and circumstance. Through the years, God has taught us how to cunningly play or sing certain chords and notes to shift atmospheres that allow the supernatural to flow freely and bring dominion in people's lives. We know that this dominion is nothing from our doing but all for God's Glory and demonstration. God desires for everyone to experience great dimensions of him, and that is the SUPERNATURAL in their lives.

We're confident believers in knowing that if you're willing; God will anoint you to move in the supernatural. Every man has an ability to worship, now what and who that worship is to; depends on the posture of the heart of mankind. So why not purely worship the divinity of our creation and in return receive the benefits of that worship – the supernatural. Wouldn't you rather worship your creator and receive the super on your natural than worship someone or something else and receive just the natural that will eventually lead to death. Whether you're worshiping God through the administration of singing, playing, speaking, or dancing; God is looking for willing vessels to demonstrate that power for miracles, signs, and wonders - are you in line!

5

The Presence - Monumental Moments

In the sacred journey of Christian worship, there are moments when the ordinary collides with the extraordinary, and the temporal touches the eternal. These are the monumental moments, instances when the presence of God is so palpable that time seems to stand still. This chapter is an exploration of those moments, those divine encounters that leave an indelible mark on the worshiper's heart.

ENCOUNTERING THE DIVINE PRESENCE

The scriptures abound with accounts of individuals who encountered the presence of God in extraordinary ways. Moses, standing before the burning bush, experienced a moment so profound that he was instructed to remove his sandals for the ground he stood on was holy (Exodus 3:5, ESV). The disciples, on the Mount of Transfiguration, witnessed the glory of Christ shining brilliantly, enveloped in the cloud of God's presence (Matthew 17:5, ESV).

In our own lives, monumental moments of encounter may not involve burning bushes or transfigured figures, but they are no less transformative and just as vital. It could be a moment of deep worship during a gathering, a quiet revelation in prayer, or an overwhelming sense of God's nearness during a time of need. These moments become monuments in our spiritual landscape, markers that remind us of the reality of the living God who meets us where we are.

THE HOLY HUSH

In the presence of God, there exists a holy hush—a stillness that descends, capturing the essence of the divine moment. It is a moment when words seem inadequate, and silence becomes a sacred language. The prophet Habakkuk captures this sense of awe, declaring, "But the Lord is in his holy temple; let all the earth keep silence before him." (Habakkuk 2:20, ESV).

Monumental moments often unfold in the midst of this holy hush, as worshipers stand in awe of the One who is present. It is in these moments that the ordinary becomes extraordinary, and the worship space transforms into holy ground.

THE COMMUNION TABLE - A MONUMENT OF UNITY

One of the most profound expressions of God's presence is found at the communion table. In the breaking of bread and the sharing of the cup, worshipers participate in a monumental moment that transcends time and space. Jesus, in instituting the Lord's Supper, said, "This is my body, which is given for you. Do this in remembrance of me." (Luke 22:19, ESV).

As we partake in the communion elements, we enter into a sacred remembrance, not merely of a historical event but of the living presence of Christ. The communion table becomes a monument of unity, a place where the worshiper encounters the presence of the risen Lord.

THE OUTPOURING OF THE HOLY SPIRIT

Another monumental moment in Christian worship is the outpouring of the Holy Spirit. The Day of Pentecost, as recorded in Acts 2, stands as a paradigmatic example. The disciples, gathered in one place, were suddenly filled with the Holy Spirit, and the sound of a rushing wind and tongues of fire marked this divine visitation.

In our worship, we anticipate and welcome the presence of the Holy Spirit. It is a moment of surrender and expectancy, a time when the ordinary is infused with the extraordinary. In the still small voice or the overwhelming flood of emotion, worshipers experience a divine encounter that leaves an indelible mark on their lives.

MONUMENTAL MOMENTS IN PERSONAL WORSHIP

Monumental moments are not confined to corporate gatherings; they are equally present in personal worship. It could be a solitary moment of prayer, a quiet reading of Scripture, or a moment of spontaneous praise. In the privacy of personal communion with God, monumental moments occur, transforming the ordinary into the extraordinary.

These moments become monuments in the landscape of the worshiper's journey, testifying to the reality of a God who is intimately involved in every aspect of our lives. They serve as reminders that the presence of God is not restricted to specific times or places but is a constant companion on our spiritual journey

OUR OXYGEN

The presence of God is our oxygen on this earth. It becomes our breath, or it is our breath. How do you think we can "instantly live" and rise from such a dead place?

In Ezekiel 37:3-6 reads "The power of the Lord came over me. The Lord brought me out by his Spirit and put me down in the middle of a valley. The valley was filled with bones. He led me all around them. I saw that there were very many bones at the bottom of the valley, and they were very dry. Then he asked me, "Son of man, can these bones live?' I answered, "Only you know, Almighty Lord." Then he said to me, "Prophesy to these bones. Tell them, 'Dry bones, listen to the Lord's word. This is what the Almighty Lord says to these bones: I will cause breath to enter you, and you will live. I will put ligaments on you, place muscles on you, and cover you with skin. I will put breath in you, and you will live. Then you will know that I am the Lord. "

Dry bones were given life once again. Something that was once dead, instantly becomes awakened by the "pneuma" from the Spirit of God.

Some Essential Key Points:

1. My responsibility to stay connected to the Spirit of God, it's mine.

2. Your own personal encounter before you can give or share with others

3. Do you value the presence of the Spirit of God? What is its value to you?

4a. Know and Understand the Spirit through the Word of God.

4b. Having a ready heart and a spirit of intercession. Allow the Spirit to make groanings for you. Scripture reference is found in Romans 8:26.

5. Take authority [begin to take as you're reading] over your relationship with God, possess it, own it.

6. Create an atmosphere for a present truth, for a right now presence of God. Having an attitude of receiving the Spirit in the moment. You can know how great our God is and also you can know how to come to the altar, but what are you going to do right then and right now! Can you still worship God? Can you worship God if there is no music, if there is music? Can you become the instrument for a moment? A worshiping tool for the Lord? Make it a moment! A moment you will never forget. A personal encounter that you will always remember.

EMBRACING MONUMENTAL MOMENTS

In our exploration of monumental moments, it is essential to recognize that they are not manufactured or conjured through human effort. They are gifts of grace, moments when God chooses to draw near and reveal His presence in a tangible way. As worshipers, our role is to cultivate an environment of receptivity, humility, and expectancy, creating space for God to move.

Whether in the collective worship of the Church or the intimate solitude of personal devotion, monumental moments are invitations to encounter the living God. They beckon us to linger in His presence, to be transformed by the glory we behold, and to carry the impact of those moments into the fabric of our daily lives.

In this chapter, we have explored the monumental moments of encountering the presence of God in Christian worship.

These moments, like monuments, stand as witnesses to the reality of a living God who draws near to His people. May we approach our worship with hearts open to these divine encounters, ready to experience the extraordinary in the midst of the ordinary, and to be forever marked by the sounds and echoes of God's presence.

6

Is My Worship Safe

In the journey of Christian worship, a question arises that delves into the security and authenticity of the worshiper's connection with the Divine. "Is My Worship Safe?" serves as an exploration into the safety of worship—both in its vulnerability and its assurance. This chapter navigates the delicate balance between a worship that embraces vulnerability before God and the safety found in the shelter of His presence.

DICTATORSHIP IN THE CHURCH

God is looking for reformers of worship, unusual people leading worship because of just needing his presence! No matter how I get it or how it comes, I want His Presence, the presence of the Lord.

I don't want to be in the midst of songs, I want to be in the midst of his glory and of his presence. We are in the midst of songs / selection, and we're not being transformed or renewed in his presence because there is no presence, no presence! Just songs...

VULNERABILITY IN WORSHIP

True worship requires vulnerability—a willingness to lay bare one's heart, doubts, fears, and joys before the Divine. The Psalms exemplify this vulnerability, with King David expressing a wide array of emotions in his worshipful songs. "Create in me a clean heart, O God, and renew a right spirit within me." (Psalm 51:10, ESV).

This chapter delves into the concept of vulnerability in worship, exploring how the act of laying one's heart before God is a genuine expression of faith. It encourages worshipers to embrace the vulnerability inherent in genuine worship, recognizing that the safety of their worship lies in the authenticity of their connection with the Divine.

SAFETY IN SURRENDER

Paradoxically, there is safety in surrender. In surrendering one's will, desires, and plans to God, the worshiper finds refuge in the assurance that God's ways are higher, and His plans are secure. Jesus, in the Garden of Gethsemane, models this profound surrender: "Not my will, but yours, be done." (Luke 22:42, ESV).

The chapter explores the safety that comes from surrendering to God, acknowledging that true worship involves **letting go of the illusion of control**. It reflects on how safety is found in entrusting one's life to the One who is both sovereign and loving.

ASSURANCE IN THE SHELTER OF HIS PRESENCE

The safety of worship is intricately tied to the presence of God. The psalmist declares, "He who dwells in the shelter of the Most High will abide in the shadow of the Almighty." (Psalm 91:1, ESV). The chapter contemplates the assurance that worshipers find in the shelter of God's presence—a haven where fears are quelled, doubts are dispelled, and faith is fortified.

As worshipers draw near to God, seeking His presence, they discover a safety that transcends circumstances. The chapter explores how the very act of being in God's presence provides a refuge—a secure place where the tumult of the world fades, and the worshiper is enveloped in peace that surpasses understanding.

THE SAFETY NET OF GRACE

Worship is not a performance but a journey, and in that journey, mistakes are inevitable. Yet, the safety of worship lies in the grace that God extends. The Apostle Paul, despite his imperfections, found solace in God's grace: "But he said to me, 'My grace is sufficient for you, for my power is made perfect in weakness.'" (2 Corinthians 12:9, ESV).

SAFETY IN COMMUNITY WORSHIP

The safety of worship extends to the community of believers. The Apostle Paul speaks of the edification that comes from corporate worship: "Let the word of Christ dwell in you richly, teaching and admonishing one another in all wisdom, singing psalms and hymns and spiritual songs, with thankfulness in your hearts to God." (Colossians 3:16, ESV). Safety is found in community worship—the shared journey, mutual encouragement, and the collective assurance that comes from worshiping together. It emphasizes the importance of fostering a worship community where individuals feel secure in expressing their hearts before God and one another.

JEREMIAH'S WARNING

Jeremiah 7:1-11 says, This is the word that came to Jeremiah from the Lord: 2 "Stand at the gate of the Lord's house and there proclaim this message: "'Hear the word of the Lord, all you people of Judah who come through these gates to worship the Lord. 3 This is what the Lord Almighty, the God of Israel, says: Reform your ways and your actions, and I will let you live in this place. 4 Do not trust in deceptive words and say, "This is the temple of the Lord, the temple of the Lord, the temple of the Lord!" 5 If you really change your ways and your actions and deal with each other justly, 6 if you do not oppress the foreigner, the fatherless or the widow and do not shed innocent blood in this place, and if you do not follow other gods to your own harm, 7 then I will let you live in this place, in the land I gave your ancestors forever and ever. 8 But look, you are trusting in deceptive words that are worthless. 9 "Will you steal and murder, commit adultery and perjury,[a] burn incense to Baal and follow other gods you have not known, 10 and then come and stand before me in this house, which bears my Name, and say, "We are safe"—safe to do all these detestable things? 11 Has this house, which bears my Name, become a den of robbers to you? But I have been watching! declares the Lord.

The Jews felt that they were safe because God was obligated to protect his temple. God's presence is not an obligation to the church. Prophet Isaiah was a warning to them about having an "attitude of safety". You are not safe w/God. Meaning, your worship is not safe. We need to begin to ask ourselves some questions?

- Is my worship safe, is it?
- Is it free from hurt, harm, injury or danger to God?
- Is it at risk?

- Is it dangerous for me or to God?
- Is my worship in trouble?

Isaiah 58 says, "Shout it aloud, do not hold back. Raise your voice like a trumpet. Declare to my people their rebellion and to the descendants of Jacob their sins. 2 For day after day they seek me out; they seem eager to know my ways, as if they were a nation that does what is right and has not forsaken the commands of its God. They ask me for just decisions and seem eager for God to come near them. 3 'Why have we fasted,' they say, and you have not seen it? Why have we humbled ourselves, and you have not noticed?' "Yet on the day of your fasting, you do as you please and exploit all your workers. 4 Your fasting ends in quarreling and strife, and in striking each other with wicked fists. You cannot fast as you do today and expect your voice to be heard on high. 5 Is this the kind of fast I have chosen, only a day for people to humble themselves? Is it only for bowing one's head like a reed and for lying in sackcloth and ashes? Is that what you call a fast, a day acceptable to the Lord? 6 "Is not this the kind of fasting I have chosen: to lose the chains of injustice and untie the cords of the yoke, to set the oppressed free and break every yoke? 7 Is it not to share your food with the hungry and to provide the poor wanderer with shelter— when you see the naked, to clothe them, and not to turn away from your own flesh and blood? 8 Then your light will break forth like the dawn, and your healing will quickly appear; then your righteousness[a] will go before you, and the glory of the Lord will be your rear guard. 9 Then you will call, and the Lord will answer; you will cry for help, and he will say: Here am I. "If you do away with the yoke of oppression, with the pointing finger and malicious talk, 10 and if you spend yourselves on behalf of the hungry and satisfy the needs of the oppressed, then your light will rise in the darkness, and your night will become like the noonday. 11 The Lord will guide you always; he will satisfy your needs in a sun-scorched land and will strengthen your frame. You will be like a well-watered garden, like a spring whose waters never fail. 12 Your people will rebuild the ancient ruins and will raise up the age-old foundations; you will be called Repairer of Broken Walls, Restorer of Streets with Dwellings. 13 "If you keep your feet from breaking the Sabbath and from doing as you please on my holy day, if you call the Sabbath a delight and the Lord's holy day honorable, and if you honor it by not going your own way and not doing as you please or speaking idle words, 14 then you will find your joy in the Lord, and I will cause you to ride in triumph on the heights of the land and to feast on the inheritance of your father Jacob." For the mouth of the Lord has spoken.

REFLECTION ON WORSHIP SAFETY

In concluding the chapter, the focus shifts to reflection, inviting worshipers to ponder the safety of their worship. It encourages self-examination, asking questions such as: How vulnerable am I in my worship? Am I finding safety in surrender? Do I seek refuge in the presence of God? Am I embracing the safety net of grace? Is my worship fostering a safe and encouraging community?

As a worshiper, reflect on these questions, they are guided to cultivate a worship that is both vulnerable and safe—a worship that reflects the authenticity of your heart and the security found in your relationship with the One who invites you to draw near with confidence and find grace in your time of need (Hebrews 4:16, ESV).

7

Is My Worship A Love Language

In the sacred tapestry of Christian worship, a thought-provoking question arises—one that reaches deep into the heart of the worshiper's relationship with God. "Is My Worship a Love Language?" serves as a contemplative exploration into the parallels between marital commitment and devotion to the Divine, unveiling the profound aspects of loyalty, intimacy, and enduring love found in both.

THE LANGUAGE THROUGH COMMITMENT

Marriage is often characterized by vows of commitment, promises of fidelity, and the covenant of love between two individuals. Similarly, worship is a language of commitment—a soul-deep declaration of allegiance, a covenant expressed through praise and adoration. The Psalms echo this sentiment: "I will bless the Lord at all times; his praise shall continually be in my mouth." (Psalm 34:1, ESV).

In the commitment of worship, the worshiper pledges allegiance to God, promising to honor and cherish the Divine in times of joy and sorrow, abundance and lack. This chapter explores the profound connection between the language of commitment in marriage and the sacred commitment expressed in worship.

INTIMACY IN WORSHIP

Just as the intimacy between spouses deepens through shared experiences, worship is a journey toward greater intimacy with God. The Bible uses the metaphor of marriage to describe the intimate relationship between God and His people. In the book of Isaiah, God says, "For your Maker is your husband, the Lord of hosts is his name; and the Holy One of Israel is Redeemer, the God of the whole earth he is called." (Isaiah 54:5, ESV).

Worship becomes a sacred space where intimacy with God is cultivated. It involves the opening of the heart, vulnerability, and a willingness to be known by the Divine. The chapter explores the parallels between the intimacy shared between spouses and the depth of connection sought in worship, emphasizing the transformative power of such intimacy in both relationships.

THE REALITY OF SACRIFICE

Marriage often requires sacrifice—of time, desires, and personal preferences. Similarly, worship involves a sacrificial offering of self. The Apostle Paul, in his letter to the Romans, speaks of presenting our bodies as living sacrifices, holy and acceptable to God, as an act of spiritual worship (Romans 12:1, ESV). The act of giving oneself becomes a sacred expression of love and devotion. It reflects on the profound truth that true worship is sacrificial, requiring a giving of the heart, mind, and soul to the One who is worthy.

ENDURING LOVE IN WORSHIP

Marriages are marked by seasons—times of joy, challenge, and growth. Similarly, worship is a lifelong journey, encompassing the highs of mountaintop experiences and the valleys of trials. The Bible speaks of God's enduring love, a love that surpasses human comprehension. "The steadfast love of the Lord never ceases; his mercies never come to an end." (Lamentations 3:22, ESV).

Enduring love in both covenant and worship, acknowledging that the journey of faith is one that unfolds over a lifetime. It reflects on the faithfulness of God and the call for worshipers to cultivate an enduring love that stands the test of time and circumstance.

THE UNITY OF TWO BECOMING ONE

In marriage, there is a profound unity where two individuals become one. Worship, likewise, is a pursuit of unity with God. The Gospel of John records Jesus' prayer for unity among believers: "that they may all be one, just as you, Father, are in me, and I in you, that they also may be in us, so that the world may believe that you have sent me." (John 17:21, ESV).

Drawing parallels between the oneness experienced in marriage and the spiritual unity sought in worship, it reflects on how worshipers through their devotion, seek a profound union with God that not only transforms individual lives but serves as a witness to the world.

REFLECTING ON THE WORSHIP LOVE LANGUAGE

As we journey through the exploration of "Is My Worship A Love Language?" the chapter concludes with reflective insights, encouraging worshipers to consider the depth of their commitment, the intimacy of their connection, the sacrificial nature of their worship, the enduring love they express, and the unity they seek in their relationship with God. It invites them to view their worship as a sacred covenant, echoing the sentiments expressed in the marriage vows, and to cultivate a devotion that mirrors the profound, enduring love found in the sacred union with the Divine.

8

Consecration & Sacrifice

In "Consecration and Sacrifice," you are invited to embark on a reflective journey, contemplating the depth and significance of consecrating yourself wholly to God and embracing sacrificial living as an act of worship. Together, let's navigate the rich biblical foundations, experience the transformative power, and discover the contemporary significance of consecration and sacrifice in our lives as worshipers.

ANSWERING THE CALL TO CONSECRATION

In the depths of our worship, we hear a resounding call to consecration—a call to set ourselves apart for the service and glory of God. The words of the Apostle Paul in Romans beckon us: "I appeal to you therefore, brothers and sisters, by the mercies of God, to present your bodies as a living sacrifice, holy and acceptable to God, which is your spiritual worship." (Romans 12:1, ESV).

This isn't just a concept; it's a personal commitment for each of us to wholeheartedly surrender to God. Together, we're exploring how this act of consecration is rooted in our desire to align every facet of our lives with the divine purpose. We reflect on the biblical examples of consecrated individuals and witness the transformative impact that consecration has on our collective journey.

SACRIFICE AS OUR ACT OF DEVOTION

Sacrifice is not a distant ritual but an integral aspect of our worship—a tangible expression of our devotion to God that involves giving up something valuable for His sake. The pages of the Bible unfold with instances of sacrificial offerings, from Abel's acceptable sacrifice to the ultimate sacrifice of Jesus on the cross.

As we dive into the nature of sacrifice in our worship, we realize it goes beyond material offerings. It encompasses the surrender of our will, desires, and ambitions, aligning them with God's purposes. Sacrifice becomes an intimate act of love and devotion that shapes our collective character and helps us prioritize the things that truly matter.

EXPERIENCING THE TRANSFORMATIVE POWER TOGETHER

We're not just going through the motions of consecration and sacrifice; we're witnessing their transformative power in our lives. Consecrating ourselves wholly to God leads to spiritual growth, renewal, and a deeper connection with the Divine. Sacrifice molds our collective character, aligning our priorities with God's kingdom values and bringing about profound changes.

Drawing on biblical narratives and the testimonies of fellow believers, we see how embracing consecration and sacrifice becomes a catalyst for transformation. It's not about perfection; it's about progress—a continuous journey of growth and renewal that we share.

BALANCING OUR PERSONAL AND COLLECTIVE CONSECRATION

While personal consecration is crucial, we also discover the significance of collective consecration within our worshiping community. Together, we commit to setting ourselves apart for God's service, fostering unity, shared purpose, and a vibrant atmosphere of consecration. The balance between our personal consecration and our communal commitment is essential for a thriving worship community.

EMBRACING THE PARADOX OF SACRIFICE TOGETHER

Sacrifice, though demanding, carries a paradoxical beauty—a divine exchange where giving leads to receiving. In relinquishing control, comfort, or material possessions in worship, we open the door for God's abundance and blessings. It's not a transaction but an expression of trust in God's faithfulness.

This paradox of sacrifice is not theoretical; it's a lived experience we share. We're learning that giving generously, even when it seems challenging, opens the floodgates of God's grace in unexpected ways.

APPLYING CONSECRATION AND SACRIFICE IN OUR EVERYDAY LIVES

As we conclude our shared journey through consecration and sacrifice, we consider how these themes find relevance in the contemporary context of our worship. Together, we explore practical ways to incorporate consecration and sacrificial living into our daily lives. Worship is not confined to specific moments but encompasses the entirety of our existence.

Through real-life examples and practical insights, we encourage each other to embrace consecration and sacrifice as ongoing, transformative aspects of our worship journey. We're called to consecrate ourselves afresh and offer sacrificial devotion as an expression of love and gratitude to the God who first loved us.

Let's define the word "Refined" - You can only be refined by fire or through the burning of fire. Dictionary.com meaning of refined is:

- To bring to fine or pure state.
- Free from impurities.
- To Purify from what is coarse, vulgar, or debasing so it has to be made through refinement back to being elegant or cultured state. Now it is polished or sophisticated.

It has experienced some things through its journey of fire. It has become more cultivated in God through life.

Maybe you have advanced in some areas in your life. You are more civilized, more courteous, more educated, more distinguished, elegant. You have received knowledge and enlightenment about the presence of God that brings out the real you, the "ethereal you" (definition: extremely delicate and light in a way that seems too perfect for this world). You have been in the smoke of God. And now you are coming out more liberal, polished, sensitive, tolerant, polite, and knowledgeable. "Up to date" - Yes lord! Amen. Hallelujah. Looking for the "new" in God. Leaving the old, mildew places, smelling like old and now you are coming out smelling like the incense of the Lord.

The aroma of change, the aroma of truth. The aroma of beauty before us. The presence of God is a place of smoke or fire. It fumigates off into other areas and places. Smoke also goes up, it elevates, it exceeds beyond.

DAVIDIC COVENANT

In this pivotal point of view, the focus is on the Davidic Covenant, a divine promise that shapes the course of biblical history and carries profound implications for the Christian understanding of worship. It begins by revisiting the covenant made between God and King David, recorded in the Old Testament. It explores the enduring significance of this covenant, wherein God pledges an everlasting dynasty for David's descendants and the establishment of an eternal kingdom.

2 Samuel 7:10 says, "I will make a place for my people Israel and plant them there. They will live in their own place and not be troubled anymore. The wicked will no longer oppress them as they used to do."

The same promise / covenant that I made with King David is established in 1 Kings 5:1-5. Then they began to build together.

9

Embodiment of God

I n this enlightening chapter, the exploration centers on the concept of the "Embodiment of God," a profound theme that resonates through the pages of the book. The chapter delves into the theological understanding of God's embodiment, not as a distant and abstract deity but as a divine reality manifest in tangible form.

In the book of psalms there were many who wrote songs and poetry within psalms. But when they were writing, they wrote with all their feelings, emotions, expressions. They offered feelings to God. It was part of their worship; it became their prayers into worship. It translated them closer to God's presence. Their feelings were expressed openly to God and before God. The human soul spoke up at that moment, that moment of anger, that moment of frustration, anxiety/fear, despair, injustice, even when they were happy.

Feelings are created by God to be used in our worship. Their feelings got them or drew them closer to God. Situations will help to emerge our true worship. They needed deliverance, rescuing, shelter, love, direction, safety, etc. God became those things to them as they worshipped/prayed in psalms. His very "Being" came to them at that time, in that moment. He became a "present help". A helper to his people (Psalms 2:7).

Let's take a look at the definition of embodiment.

Embodiment: a tangible or visible form, manifestation, personification, [His person himself comes in your space], His model, essence [the real thing], realization...

Embodiment in the Greek [Strongs 2320] [The personal God], the Godhead, the Triune Being: Father/Son/Holy Spirit.

Colossians 2:9-10 says, "All of God lives in Christ's body, and God has made you complete in Christ. Christ is in charge of every ruler and authority." The morphosis (process of forming or shaping) of his presence before me.

As this chapter concludes, we encourage you to continue in a profound invitation to embrace the idea of the Embodiment of God as a central and vibrant aspect of your faith.

10

At The Gates

True Worshipers At The Gates of Cities
John 4: 23-24 (Worship in Spirit & Truth)

Your worship doesn't just manifest for your own life & family. Your worship is also used to help affect your city, region & nation.

Acts 14:19-20 AMP - "But Jews arrived from Antioch and Iconium, and having won over the crowds, they stoned Paul and dragged him out of the city, thinking he was dead. But the disciples formed a circle around him, and he got up and went back into the city; and the next day he went on with Barnabas to Derbe."

Why did the Jews want to stone Paul & remove him from the city of Lystra?

Let's hit the rewind button and back up some verses to see the reason why and how the shift of true worship affected a city....

Acts 14:8-18 AMP - "Now at Lystra a man sat who was unable to use his feet, for he was crippled from birth and had never walked. This man was listening to Paul as he spoke, and Paul looked intently at him and saw that he had faith to be healed, and said with a loud voice, "Stand up on your feet." And he jumped up and began to walk. And the crowds, when they saw what Paul had done, raised their voices, shouting in the Lycaonian language, "The gods have come down to us in human form!" They began calling Barnabas, Zeus [chief of the Greek gods], and Paul, Hermes [messenger of the Greek gods], since he took the lead in speaking. The priest of Zeus, whose temple was at the entrance of the city, brought bulls and garlands to the city gates, and wanted to offer sacrifices with the crowds. But when the apostles Barnabas and Paul heard about it, they tore their robes and rushed out into the crowd, shouting, "Men, why are you doing these things? We too are only men of the same nature as you, bringing the good news to you, so that you turn from these useless and meaningless things to the living God, who made the heaven and the earth and the sea and everything that is in them. In generations past He permitted all the nations to go their own ways; yet He did not leave Himself without some witness [as evidence of Himself], in that He kept constantly doing good things and showing you kindness, and giving you rains from heaven and productive seasons, filling your hearts with food and happiness." Even saying these words, with difficulty they prevented the people from offering sacrifices to them."

Paul & Barnabas true worship of spirit & truth led the people to shift their worship and offering of sacrifices from their old gods to the Living God. This was such a tremendous shift in the city of Lystra that Jews from other regions had to come and stone Paul. But what the stoners didn't know was that the effect of true worship was already embedded in the city. Now we're going to fast forward to versus 21-23 to see the outcome....

Acts 14:21-23 AMP - "They preached the good news to that city and made many disciples, then they returned to Lystra and to Iconium and to Antioch, strengthening and establishing the hearts of the disciples; encouraging them to remain firm in the faith, saying, "It is through many tribulations and hardships that we must enter the kingdom of God." When they had appointed elders for them in every church, having prayed with fasting, they entrusted them to the Lord in whom they believed [and joyfully accepted as the Messiah]."

Isn't this amazing that after the shift of a city worship; that discipleship was able to be released and Kingdom advancement of establishing elders was manifested.

Right NOW, ministry & community leaders are desiring their cities to shift from the false to the truth; from poverty to wealth; from violence to peace; from lack to abundance. Well, can we tell you that it involves your worship. Worshipping the TRUE AND LIVING GOD in spirit & truth! There are city gates that are about to shift to God's people releasing worship gatherings & revelation teachings on worship. These city gates are going to be directed and guarded spiritually by true worshippers; who will only allow the true & pure to enter the city. Revival is going to engulf those cities and an entire city will be influenced by true worshippers!

11

Habitation

Let's take a look at the definition of habitat.....

1. A person's usual or preferred surroundings
2. The natural home/environment of an animal, plant, or organism.

In Jeremiah 3:1-7, God says, You can "live" where I "live," you can dwell in this place and stay here with me. But only if you change:

1. Your Ways
2. Your Behavior

Practice this way, my way and practice, get in the habit of the new disciplines and you can stay here with me. God will "appoint" a place for people that are willing to surrender and willing to take chances and risk on His behalf. People that want to be filled with Him to dwell in such a place. This is Gods covenant with David, and this is His covenant with us. David's desire but Solomon's destiny to build for the Lord, a place for Him to dwell among them.

The heartbeat of worship is directly sent and released from the heart and mind of God. A flowing stream of sound and frequency is the very communication that is released from heaven to earth to man from God. Creating and hearing sounds, patterns, rhythms, and expressions from what is being transcribed and resounded in heaven is echoed onto the earth! The sound is created to bring influence to the atmosphere, of the space, or wherever. Certain sounds of heartbeat can bring a rapid, vivid, and warlike sound, a sound of cheer and praise and excitement, or it can put you in a state of rest/ease in the Lord. Certain sounds filter through the very soul (mind, will, and emotions) of man. Heavenly heartbeats can bring deliverance, healing, and break and shatter curses, sickness and disease in someone's body!! Listen for the sound and allow it to penetrate and flow and filter down from heaven onto the earth to show forth demonstration and power of an atmosphere built and created from heaven onto earth. Passion and intimacy are what God is looking for in worship. There is a participation and engagement that heaven longs for people to have to release the fullness of His glory on the earth!!! Our worship here on earth is preparation for worship in Heaven. We got to catch it here first!!!

Here are a few more scriptures:

Psalms 34:3 - "O magnify the Lord with me, And let us exalt His name together!"

Psalms 95:6 - "Come, let us worship and bow down, Let us kneel before the Lord our Maker"

Psalms 66:4 - "All the earth will worship You, And will sing praises to You; They will sing praises to Your name." Selah"

Ephesians 5:19 - "speaking to one another in psalms and hymns and spiritual songs, singing and making melody with your heart to the Lord"

Psalms 22:27 - "All the ends of the earth will remember and turn to the Lord, And all the families of the nations will worship before You."

12

Which Court Are You In

Which Court Are You In: Outer Court / Inner Court / Holy of Holies

The Tabernacle and its courts represent the three main parts of man and its functions. **The Outer Court represent the body, the Holy Place represents the soul, and the Holy of Holies represent the spirit.** The word holy simply means "different" or even "set apart." However, our human nature is physical and visual, so God did give the Israelites an object that would help them to know and be aware of His presence among them—the tabernacle (a tent that served as a portable temple).

The entire tabernacle was holy and in that it was set apart for worship and sacrifices to God. However, the tabernacle was divided into 3 sections, the Outer Court, the Holy Place, and the Most Holy Place (or Holy of Holies). The priest and Levites ministered in the section of the outer courts as they offered sacrifices for guilt and sin as well as the other sacrifices. In the center of the Outer Court was a tent that only the priests could enter. This place was set apart and it was a very holy place. At the back of the Holy Place was a smaller chamber called the Holy of Holies or

Most Holy Place. Within this smaller chamber was the ark of the covenant.

It's so important that we understand which court do we really exist in? Existence is vital to God when it comes to us because it's the ultimate reason why He made us to exist and dwell with Him. To build a companionship and friendship with Him through worship and communication to Him. We must enter through and get to where the best of God is and that is the Holy of Holies. We can enter, freely now, not through animal sacrifice but through the new covenant given through the blood and atonement of Jesus Christ our Savior. We must always remember that the veil in the temple was torn down for us that humanity unfit for the presence of God, flesh can't glory in House or His Presence. Sin offerings were offered annually and numerous times a day on a daily basis. Other sacrifices repeated daily showed graphically that sin could not truly be atoned for or erased by mere animal sacrifices. Jesus Christ, through His death, has removed the barriers between God and man, and now we may approach Him with confidence and boldness.

13

Mountain of Worship (Religion)

The mountain of worship usually requires something that you do not want to give up. It is what you need to get to the next pinnacle place.

After the place of the Pinnacle comes the timing of fame. It will spread throughout the regions.

Christ was known and famous for releasing healing and deliverance with and around the regions. He cast out demons and cured various diseases.

Mark 1:21-28 says, "They went to Capernaum, and when the Sabbath came, Jesus went into the synagogue and began to teach. The people were amazed at his teaching, because he taught them as one who had authority, not as the teachers of the law. Just then a man in their synagogue who was possessed by an impure spirit cried out, what do you want with us, Jesus of Nazareth? Have you come to destroy us? I know who you are—the Holy One of God!" Be quiet!" said Jesus sternly. "Come out of him!" The impure spirit shook the man violently and came out of him with a shriek. The people were all so amazed that they asked each other, "What is this? A new teaching—and with authority! He even gives orders to impure spirits, and they obey him." News about him spread quickly over the whole region of Galilee."

Get ready to be used for miracles, signs, and wonders.

If you read Exodus 17, you will find that murmuring, faultfinding, and complaining took the Israelites out of the will of God. If we're not careful this can happen in our Households and Churches.

Moses, Aaron, and the Israelites dealt with the wilderness desert; being "thirsty."

There was a want for water, and they were being tested and tempted in this place of Massah. They were on trial with and before God.

Another similar place called Meribah; which means "contention" & "strife". A place of quarreling and provoked anger. The people were tempted because they were nearly close to stoning their overseer and only because they were mad at him for not fulfilling their personal wishes and wants. It caused them to not only come against Moses but to really come against God; whom Moses represented for the people. Because Moses did not give them what they wanted, they almost believed that the Lord does not bring aid to His own. These ill-willed feelings provoked God to anger, and the people were now in trouble with God and caused a quarrel, a fight, strife and contention with Him. And these spirits of contention, quarreling, fighting, and strife was also released around the camp as well.

This type of behavior is so important to understand, that Paul uses it in 1Corinthians 10:1-12 (KJV); when dealing with the Corinthian church.

14

Glory Pinnacle

This completes the testing

Satan wants you to destroy yourself (physically, character, your influence, etc.). He wants you to get rid of yourself and get off of the scene, out of the picture.

Psalm 91:11,12 says, "For he will command his angels concerning you to guard you in all your ways; they will lift you up in their hands, so that you will not strike your foot against a stone."

The angels are coming to rescue and preserve you, to keep you in obedience and service for you. In times of pressure and temptation you need to rest in your angels' hands and stay preserved in obedience. Ask the Lord to watch over me and guard my soul. I will reach the next level of glory. The Holy Spirit will carry me to that place of consoling and comfort. You should stay there until you are through that pressured place that will take you to glory. The angels will assist us and minister to us. This is confirmed in Hebrews 1:14 where it says, "Are not all angels ministering spirits sent to serve those who will inherit salvation?"

15

Journey of Worship: A Closing Reflection

As we reach the final chapter of our exploration in "Here Comes the Bride," it is a moment to pause, reflect, and offer a closing reflection on the profound journey of worship we have undertaken together. This chapter serves as a heartfelt conclusion, weaving together the themes, insights, and transformative moments encountered throughout the book.

GRATITUDE FOR THE JOURNEY

First and foremost, let us express gratitude for the journey we've shared—a journey into the depths of worship, the exploration of sacred concepts, and the unveiling of the Divine in various facets of our lives. In the tapestry of worship, every thread has contributed to the richness of our understanding and experience.

A TAPESTRY WOVEN WITH THREADS OF WORSHIP

Our exploration has taken us through diverse landscapes—the consecrated moments of surrender, the heights of intimate connection with God, the sacred spaces we inhabit, and the transformative power of consecration and sacrifice. Each chapter has been a thread intricately woven, creating a beautiful and diverse mosaic of worship.

ACKNOWLEDGING THE DIVINE PRESENCE

Throughout our journey, the constant refrain has been the acknowledgment of the Divine Presence—whether in the echoes of the Davidic Covenant, the contemplation of God's embodiment, or the recognition of the Divine Habitat. In every chapter, we have glimpsed the ever-present God inviting us into a deeper communion.

EMBRACING THE SACRED METAPHOR

As we conclude this book, let us reflect on the overarching metaphor—the bride and the bridegroom. This sacred imagery calls us to embrace a relationship with God that mirrors the intimacy, commitment, and joy found in the covenant of marriage. It invites us to be the bride eagerly anticipating the arrival of the Bridegroom, our Lord and Savior.

A CALL TO CONTINUED REFLECTION

This closing chapter is not an end but a transition—a call to continued reflection on the themes presented. As readers, may you carry the insights gained into your personal journey of worship. Allow the truths uncovered to permeate your daily life, influencing the way you approach God, your fellow believers, and the world around you.

INVITATION TO WORSHIP

In closing, we extend an invitation—a call to worship. Let the awareness of God's presence permeate your thoughts, actions, and aspirations. In your worship, may you find renewal, transformation, and a deepening of your relationship with the Lord. The journey of worship does not cease with the last page but continues as a dynamic and ongoing expression of our faith.

May the words penned in these chapters resonate in your hearts, and may your worship be a fragrant offering, a melody of devotion, and a dance of joy before the King. As you close this book, may you carry the echoes of worship with you, and may the Bridegroom's presence accompany you on the path ahead.

In the name of the Father, the Son, and the Holy Spirit. Amen.

Thank You

To every reader who has journeyed through these pages with us—**thank you**.

Thank you for opening your heart, for leaning in, and for allowing us to share this sacred space with you. It is our deepest prayer that something within these words stirred your spirit, confirmed your calling, and deepened your desire to worship the Father in Spirit and in Truth.

We do not take it lightly that you chose to walk this journey with us. Your hunger for God, your pursuit of His presence, and your commitment to Kingdom living inspire us more than you know.

To all who have prayed for us, supported us, believed in us, and continue to stand with us—we honor you. Your love and encouragement fuel the flame of this ministry.

May your life be marked by fresh encounters, holy fire, and the undeniable presence of the Bridegroom. We bless you as you carry worship forward in your own unique way.

With all our love and gratitude,
Apostles Lamont & Tiffany Bigham

About the Authors

Apostles Lamont & Tiffany Bigham are visionary leaders, prophetic voices, and passionate worshipers with a global mandate to advance the Kingdom of God. Together, they co-founded City Worship Church in Maryland and Mont & Tiff Ministries, an International movement dedicated to empowering believers in worship, leadership, marriage, and deliverance.

Widely known as Apostle Mont and Apostle Tiff, they are each uniquely anointed—with Apostle Lamont carrying a revelatory teaching gift and a regional worship sound that shifts atmospheres, and Apostle Tiffany known for her prophetic accuracy, spontaneous song, and Spirit-led insight that guides people into their God-ordained "next." With over two decades of ministry experience, they are committed to cultivating environments where lives are healed, souls are strengthened, and worship becomes a doorway to transformation.

Their shared heart beats for holistic restoration—spirit, soul, and body. Whether through music, mentorship, or the Word, they are devoted to seeing individuals and communities walk in clarity, freedom, and divine identity.